GW00691834

grill pan cooking

RYLAND
PETERS
& SMALL
LONDON NEW YORK

elsa petersen-schepelern

photography by peter cassidy

grill pan cooking

First published in Great Britain in 2001 as *Grill Pan Cooking*
This paperback edition first published in 2006
by Ryland Peters & Small
20–21 Jockey's Fields
London WC1R 4BW
www.rylandpeters.com

10 9 8 7 6 5 4 3 2 1

Text © Elsa Petersen-Schepelern 2001, 2006
Design and photographs © Ryland Peters & Small 2001, 2006

Printed and bound in China

The author's moral rights have been asserted. All rights reserved. No part
of this publication may be reproduced, stored in a retrieval system or
transmitted in any form or by any means, electronic, mechanical,
photocopying or otherwise, without the prior permission of the publisher.

ISBN-10: 1 84597 157 4
ISBN-13: 978 1 84597 157 1

A catalogue record for this book is available from the British Library.

Author's acknowledgements

My thanks to my sister Kirsten, Peter Bray and Luc Votan. Thanks also to
Sheridan Lear the 'Preserving Princess' and Maddie Bastianelli, as ever.
Thanks also to the brilliant Louise Pickford for her beautiful food styling,
to photographer Peter Cassidy who just takes my breath away, to stylist
Helen Trent and to Louise Leffler for her brilliant design, as usual. Thanks
also to Kara Kara of Pond Place and the Conran Shop in Fulham Road,
both in South Kensington, for lending us their gorgeous props.

Senior Designer   Louise Leffler
Designer   Luis Peral-Aranda
Editor   Maddalena Bastianelli
Production   Meryl Silbert
Art Director   Gabriella Le Grazie
Publishing Director   Alison Starling

Food Stylist   Louise Pickford
Stylist   Helen Trent
Photographer's Assistant   Rachel Tomlinson

contents

all the fun of a barbecue without having to light a fire...

Stove-top grill pans give the flavour of a barbecue without all the smoke and the bugs! If there's just one or two of you, and it's a weeknight, and you've just arrived home from work, the grill pan is exactly what's needed. With today's obsession with low-fat, fast-cooked food, this clever little pan is just perfect. It raises the food up and out of the fat and it cooks through quicker than almost any other method. Then there's the bonus that all those toasty bits are utterly delicious!

When is a pan not a griddle?

The stove-top grill pan is sometimes called a griddle. They're close relations, but a griddle has a flat surface, while our beloved pan has ridges. (A griddle was used by old-time Scottish cooks to bake scones on top of the fire, because they didn't have ovens.)

Grill pan rules

• Heat the pan over a medium heat until it reaches the required temperature before you add the food.

• Oil the food, not the pan. (Though I defy anyone not to add just a little olive oil now and then.)

• When you add the food, leave it there. Don't move it around. When it's ready, it will move without sticking.

• Cook one side of the food thoroughly – so that the second side will need less time. This way, you can add spice rubs to the second side and the spices will be less likely to burn.

• To make sure thicker foods, such as poultry, cook right through and are properly in contact with the surface, put a weight on top. I use a saucepan half-filled with water.

• Cool the pan before running under hot water to remove the major particles. Then wash in the normal way – remembering that if the surface is non-stick or cast iron it shouldn't go in the dishwasher (at least not unless the manufacturer's instructions say it's OK).

• If it's cast iron, don't use soap on it, just lots of hot water and a scrubbing brush. Make sure the pan is dried thoroughly – I always dry it over a gentle heat on the stove for a minute or so – then rub it over with some kitchen paper dipped in olive oil.

• Buy the biggest pan you can find – then you'll be able to cook a few grilled vegetables at the same time as the meat, fish, or poultry – or even 2 whole fishes. The results are always delicious and crispy.

Best wishes and great grilling!

500 g asparagus tips
   (don't choose very thin ones)
2 tablespoons peanut oil
2 garlic cloves, crushed
3 cm fresh ginger, peeled and grated
sea salt

Lemon-soy butter
4 tablespoons unsalted butter
3 spring onions, finely sliced
3 cm fresh ginger, grated and juice squeezed
1 teaspoon Szechuan peppercorns, coarsely
   crushed, or Japanese 7-spice (*sichimi*
   togarishi) or freshly ground black pepper
2 tablespoons white rice vinegar
freshly squeezed juice of ½ lemon
4 tablespoons sake or mirin (Japanese
   rice wine)
1 tablespoon soy sauce, preferably Japanese
Serves 4

Asparagus, the original finger food, is good to serve at a party – one of the few things that you should eat with your fingers (so don't put any dressing on the blunt end!)

To make the Lemon-soy Butter, melt the butter in a small saucepan, add the remaining ingredients and bring to the boil. Boil fiercely for 1 minute, then remove from the heat and keep the mixture warm.

To prepare the asparagus, put the peanut oil, garlic, ginger and sea salt in a plastic bag, then add the asparagus and toss gently to coat.

Heat a stove-top grill pan, add the asparagus and cook for 2 minutes on each side until barely cooked. Arrange on a platter, and pour the Lemon-soy Butter over the pointy ends or serve in a small bowl.

vegetables and cheese

char-grilled asparagus
with lemon-soy butter

4 corn cobs
1 tablespoon corn oil or peanut oil
1 tablespoon chilli oil
juice of 1 lime

Salsa
2 red chillies, halved and deseeded
2 red peppers, halved and deseeded
2 red onions, coarsely chopped
1 ripe mango or ½ papaya (optional), peeled,
** deseeded and chopped into 1 cm dice**
1 garlic clove, crushed
4 tablespoons sunflower oil
juice of 1 lime
a large bunch of coriander leaves, chopped
sea salt and freshly ground black pepper
Serves 4

If the corn is unhusked, tie back the husks to use as a handle and remove and discard the silk. Mix the corn oil and chilli oil together and brush all over the corn*.

Heat a grill pan over medium heat until hot. Add the corn cobs and cook, turning frequently, until golden brown and lightly charred all over, about 8 minutes. Remove from the pan and put on a plate to cool. Sprinkle with the lime juice.

To make the salsa, add the chillies to the pan and cook until lightly charred. Chop the flesh into small dice. Peel the peppers with a vegetable peeler and dice the flesh. Cut the kernels off the corn cobs and put in a shallow dish. Add the peppers and chillies, the chopped onion, diced mango or papaya and crushed garlic. Add the sunflower oil, lime juice, salt and pepper and toss well. Add the chopped coriander leaves, toss and serve with grilled fish, chicken or meats.

*If serving the cobs only, par-boil them first until almost tender, then serve with butter melted with sliced or crushed chillies.

Char-grilled corn is popular all over the world. I've seen it in Pakistan, boiled first, then cooked over the coals. Lovely with melted butter and a sprinkle of chilli. Eat the grilled cobs as they are, or mix the kernels with other grilled or uncooked vegetables and fruit to make a smoky, spicy salsa.

char-grilled corn salsa

pan-grilled bruschetta

1 large loaf Italian bread, such as pugliese or ciabatta
1 whole head of garlic
extra virgin olive oil

Serves 4

Cut the top off the head of garlic and rub it all over the loaf of bread. Cut the loaf into thick slices, about 2 cm. Crush one of the cloves into a small bowl and add about 125 ml olive oil. Stir well, then smear the flavoured oil roughly over the bread with a pastry brush. Heat a stove-top grill pan over medium heat until hot. Add the bread and cook until golden and barred with brown. Keep warm in the oven while you prepare the toppings.

Char-grilled Courgettes with Parsley Oil

Courgettes are great grilled – the charred bits have a wonderful smoky flavour and the vegetable itself stays crisp. Try a mixture of green and yellow courgettes and use on bruschetta, as an antipasto, as a salad, or with meat, fish or poultry.

500 g medium or baby courgettes
3 tablespoons olive oil
1 mozzarella cheese, pulled into shreds
cherry or mini plum tomatoes, halved
sea salt and coarsely cracked black pepper

Parsley Oil
a large bunch of parsley, with stalks, coarsely chopped
250 ml extra virgin olive oil
a pinch of salt

Serves 4

To make the Parsley Oil, put the parsley in a food processor and chop for about 30 seconds. Gradually add the olive oil and keep working to form a green purée. Add a pinch of salt and purée again. Set aside, preferably overnight in the refrigerator, but for at least 30 minutes, to develop flavour and colour. Strain through a fine nylon sieve into a jug or bowl and use for this and other recipes.

To cook the courgettes, cut them lengthways into 5 mm slices. Put in a plastic bag, add the olive oil, salt and pepper and shake to coat. Heat a stove-top grill pan over medium heat until hot, add the courgette slices and cook for about 2 minutes on each side until barred with brown and cooked through but not wilted.

Arrange on the bruschetta with the mozzarella pieces and halved cherry tomatoes. Drizzle with Parsley Oil, sprinkle with salt and pepper and serve.

The courgettes may also be used as part of the antipasto on page 16 or to accompany other dishes.

Other toppings

Char-grilled Peppers (page 15) with Parma ham and basil leaves. Drizzle with basil oil, made in the same way as Parsley Oil (above).

Char-grilled Aubergines (page 16) with feta cheese and sprigs of oregano. Arrange the aubergine slices in loops on top of the bruschetta, top with toasted pine nuts, add the feta, drizzle with olive oil and serve.

Bruschetta is marvellous cooked on the grill pan. Not only do you achieve attractive barred toast marks on your bread, but you get a delightfully smoky flavour too. Use the best-quality extra virgin olive oil you can find – this is a way to show off great ingredients. I use a small whole head of garlic with the top lopped off, just because it's easier to handle. I use so much garlic in other dishes that the rest of the cloves are used in no time. Use a single clove only if you're feeling frugal. Add your favourite toppings.

grilled polenta with grilled peppers

Use quick-cook polenta to save time, and use any of the char-grilled vegetables mentioned in the previous recipe.

Prepare the polenta according to the packet instructions, stir in the butter, then pour into the oiled cake tin. Let cool and set. Chill until ready to grill. (This step can be done the day before.)

To make the Basil Oil, put the basil in a food processor and pulse until finely chopped. Add the oil gradually through the feed tube, then add a pinch of salt. Chill for at least 30 minutes, or preferably overnight to intensify flavour and colour. Strain through a nylon sieve or a tea strainer into a jug.

To cook the peppers, put the halves or pieces in a plastic bag, add the olive oil, salt and pepper and shake to coat with oil. Heat a stove-top grill pan over medium heat until hot. Add the peppers, skin side down, put a heavy weight, such as a large saucepan, on top and cook until dark and charred with marks. Turn the pieces over, put the saucepan back on top and cook until tender. Use as is, or, to remove the skins, transfer the peppers to a small saucepan and put on the lid – the skins will gently steam off and you won't lose any of the delicious juices.

Turn the polenta out of the cake tin and cut into 8 wedges. Reheat the grill pan, then brush the polenta wedges with olive oil, add to the pan and cook until barred with brown on one side. Turn the pieces over and cook the other side until hot, golden and browned. Transfer to heated plates, top with the peppers, drizzle with Basil Oil and any pepper juices, add sprigs of basil and oregano and serve.

1 packet quick-cook polenta, about 100 g
2 tablespoons butter
sea salt and freshly ground black pepper

Char-grilled peppers
6 red or yellow peppers, preferably long peppers, halved and deseeded
olive oil, for coating
sea salt and freshly ground black pepper
sprigs of basil and oregano, to serve

Basil oil
1 large bunch of basil
125 ml extra virgin olive oil
sea salt

1 springform cake tin, oiled
Serves 8

grilled italian antipasto

A combination of the char-grilled vegetables in this chapter.

2 long red peppers, halved and
   deseeded
2 long yellow or orange peppers,
   halved and deseeded, with
   stems intact if possible
2 red chillies, halved and
   deseeded (optional)
4 medium yellow courgettes
4 medium green courgettes
4 long narrow aubergines or
   8 small Japanese aubergines
4 sprigs of thyme or oregano,
   chopped

Marinade
500 ml virgin olive oil
125 ml white wine vinegar
sea salt and whole black
   peppercorns, crushed
small sprigs of thyme or oregano

Serves 8

Following the previous recipe, pan-grill the peppers
and either use as is, or remove the skins. Grill the chillies,
if using, in the same way as the peppers, then slice
lengthways into fine strips. Grill the courgettes as
described on page 12.

To prepare the aubergines, cut them lengthways into
1 cm slices, put in a plastic bag, add the olive oil, salt
and pepper, shake to coat, then pan-grill as in the recipe
for grilled peppers on the previous page. Put all the
vegetables in separate containers.

To make the marinade, put the oil, vinegar, salt, pepper
and thyme or oregano in a small saucepan and heat,
stirring. Remove from the heat and carefully add the
vinegar (take care or the oil may spatter). Pour over the
vegetables. Let marinate for at least 30 minutes, then serve.

Alternatively, they may be packed into jars, covered with
the olive oil mixture and refrigerated. When ready to
serve, let return to room temperature first.

Choose one or more of these delicious vegetables to accompany other dishes. Cook with olive oil if serving with western foods, or peanut oil if serving with Asian dishes.

grilled pumpkin, sweet potato and plantain

If using plantains, cut them in half lengthways. Using a small, sharp knife, cut out the seeds in a long strip. You can cook the plantains in their skins, or remove them.

2 green plantains (optional)

500 g pumpkin or butternut, peeled, deseeded and cut in 1 cm slices

2 orange sweet potatoes, peeled and cut in 1 cm slices

4 tablespoons olive oil or peanut oil

sea salt and freshly ground black pepper

Serves 4

Put the plantains, pumpkin or butternut and sweet potatoes in a plastic bag, sprinkle with olive or peanut oil, salt and pepper and shake until well coated – add extra oil if necessary.

Heat a stove-top grill pan over medium heat until hot and arrange the slices of vegetable on top. Grill at a medium heat for about 5 minutes on one side until barred with brown. Carefully turn over with a fish slice and cook the other side for another 5 minutes or until cooked through. If cooking in batches, transfer to a heatproof plate and keep warm in the oven.

Serve with meats, fish, poultry or vegetarian dishes.

char-grilled yoghurt cheese

Paneer is a marvellous cheese for cooking. If you're lucky enough to live near an Indian supermarket, you'll be able to buy it, but if not, make it yourself using the recipe below. It's incredibly easy to make, and even the hard variety used in this only takes about 5 hours. Start it the night before and leave it overnight in the fridge to firm up. This makes excellent party food too. Thanks to my friends Usha and Mittal in Agra, whose recipe this is.

Brush the paneer, haloumi or provolone cheese with oil. Heat a stove-top grill pan over medium heat. Add the cubes of cheese and char-grill until lightly brown on all sides. Mix the sea salt and chilli powder or paprika together in a small bowl and sprinkle over the cheese. Serve warm or cool, with drinks.

* Note: To make your own paneer, put 1 litre milk in a saucepan, bring to the boil, then stir in 2 tablespoons fresh lemon juice and 2 tablespoons plain yoghurt. When the milk curdles, ladle it gently into a sieve lined with muslin set over a bowl. Let drain for about 3 hours and discard the whey (or use it for baking). Fold the muslin over the top of the cheese, put a plate on top and a heavy food can on top of that to weight it down. Put in the refrigerator overnight – you'll have paneer in the morning. For even firmer cheese, keep it weighted in the refrigerator for a further 1–2 days.

500 g paneer (see note*), haloumi or
    provolone cheese, cut into 2 cm cubes
peanut or mustard oil, for brushing

To serve
1 tablespoon sea salt
1 teaspoon chilli powder or hot paprika
Serves 10 as finger food

fish and seafood

japanese salt-grilled salmon

A semi-sashimi. Salting before cooking is a wonderful Japanese cooking technique. It removes some of the fishy odours and also brings the fish oils to the surface, so the skin is crisp and delicious. Try it with other recipes – not just Japanese.

8 small salmon fillets, skin on
sea salt
peanut oil, for brushing

To serve
2 lemons, cut in wedges
4 teaspoons wasabi paste
2 tablespoons Japanese pink
 pickled ginger
chives (optional)

Serves 4

Put a layer of salt on a plate, then add the salmon, skin side down. Set aside for 20 minutes, then rinse off the salt and pat the fish dry.

Heat a stove-top grill pan to medium heat. Brush the fish with peanut oil or put it in a plastic bag, add a few tablespoons of the peanut oil, shake gently to coat, then remove the fish from the bag.

Put the fish on the pan, skin side down. Let cook without moving for about 5 minutes. The top of the fish will exude drops of water and the skin will be crisp.

If serving rare, remove the fish from the heat, then serve with lemon, wasabi, pink pickled ginger and a few chives, if using.

If you prefer to cook the fish further, turn it over and cook for about 1 minute more.

4 cod steaks about 250 g each

1 tablespoon rice vinegar

leaves from 2 whole bok choy, separated
   and rinsed

Japanese marinade*

4 tablespoons tamari (Japanese soy sauce)

4 tablespoons mirin (Japanese rice wine)

1 tablespoon sake

2 tablespoons peanut oil, plus extra for
   brushing

Serves 4

* If preferred, use a Western-style marinade
instead: mix 4 tablespoons olive oil or basil oil
(page 12) with 1 tablespoon white wine, 1 red
onion, finely chopped, 2 garlic cloves, crushed,
½ teaspoon salt and 1 tablespoon black peppercorns,
crushed. In addition, 2 tablespoons chopped fresh
herbs, such as marjoram, may also be added.

Cod, monkfish or any other thick, meaty fish
is good this way. This is also my favourite
way with bok choy – the contrast between
the wilted greens and the crisp, crunchy
stems is delicious.

Fill a wide, shallow dish with water and add the rice vinegar. Add the
pieces of cod and soak for 2 minutes. Drain and pat dry with kitchen
paper. Put the tamari, mirin, sake and peanut oil in the dish, stir well,
then add the fish, turning until well coated with the mixture. Set
aside for up to 30 minutes, if time allows.

Heat a stove-top grill pan over medium heat until hot. Add the fish,
skin side down, then cook for about 5 minutes or until beads of
moisture appear on the top of the fish. Baste the fish with the tamari
mixture, turn it over and cook for another 2 minutes or until the fish
feels firm to the touch: the time will depend on the thickness of the
fish – do not overcook. Boil the marinade in a small saucepan.

Remove the fish to a plate and keep warm, then rinse the pan, pat
dry, then reheat and brush with oil (this is one of the few times you
oil the pan, and not the food). Add the bok choy and cook until the
leaves are wilted and the stems hot but still firm.

Serve the fish and bok choy on heated plates and drizzle with a
spoonful of the boiled marinade.

grilled cod with grilled bok choy

moroccan sardines

Chermoula is a ubiquitous fish marinade from Morocco. I have put it with sardines, because they are tiny, quick to cook, healthy and oily, so you don't have to worry about them sticking to the pan. However any fish will do – even white fish, though you will have to add more oil. If you don't have time for the chermoula, just brush with harissa paste thinned with lemon juice.

12 sardines, cleaned
4 lemons, cut into 5 mm slices
olive oil, for brushing

Chermoula
1 teaspoon cumin seeds
2 teaspoons coriander seeds
a large bunch of coriander, including stems
**   and roots if possible**
leaves from a large bunch of mint
leaves from a large bunch of flat leaf parsley
1 teaspoon Spanish paprika
½ teaspoon turmeric
2.5 cm fresh ginger, peeled and grated
4 garlic cloves, crushed
2 small onions, finely chopped
3 red chillies, deseeded and finely chopped
juice of 2 lemons
125 ml extra virgin olive oil

Serves 4

To make the chermoula, put the cumin and coriander seeds in a small frying pan and stir-fry until aromatic, about 1 minute. Do not let burn. Cool and crush to a powder with a mortar and pestle.

Chop the fresh coriander coarsely (leaves, stems and roots if possible) and put in a food processor. Add the parsley and mint leaves and blend until finely chopped. Add the toasted and crushed seeds and all the other chermoula ingredients and blend to a paste. Transfer to a jar or bowl, cover with clingfilm and chill overnight.

Next day, spread the paste over a shallow dish and arrange the sardines on top. Put 1 teaspoon chermoula in each cavity and spread the remainder over the top. Sprinkle with salt and pepper, then cover and chill for at least 30 minutes or up to 1 hour.

When ready to cook, transfer the fish to a heated stove-top grill pan and cook for about 2 minutes on each slide.

At the same time, brush the lemons with olive oil, then add to the pan and grill until charred.

Serve the sardines with the lemons. A watercress salad would be a delicious accompaniment.

Char-grilling is a perfect treatment for big, meaty fish such as swordfish or tuna. This smoked tomato sauce is my greatest invention – you'll want to make it in quantity and freeze for other uses, so smoke multiple quantities of the tomatoes in tiered metal Chinese steamers instead of on a rack.

tuna with tea-smoked tomato sauce

4 fresh tuna steaks, 3 cm thick
125 ml olive oil
1 tablespoon freshly ground
    black pepper
4 large garlic cloves, finely sliced
500 g canned cannellini beans,
    lightly crushed with a fork
sea salt and freshly ground black
    pepper
salad leaves, to serve

Tea-smoked tomatoes
8 tablespoons leaf tea, such as
    Lapsang Souchong
2 tablespoons plain flour
1 tablespoon brown sugar
zest from 1 orange, removed
    with a vegetable peeler
4–6 green cardamom pods,
    crushed
2 red onions, cut in 6 wedges
4 large garlic cloves, halved
    lengthways
12 plum tomatoes, halved
sea salt flakes, to taste

Serves 4

Heat the olive oil, pepper and garlic in a saucepan until hot but not smoking. Infuse for at least 10 minutes. Reserve 2–3 tablespoons of the oil and transfer the rest to a wide, shallow dish. Add the tuna and turn to coat. Set aside for 30 minutes or overnight in the refrigerator.

To prepare the tomatoes, line a wok with foil, add the tea leaves, flour, sugar, orange peel and cardamom pods. Put a round rack about 3 cm above the mixture. Add the onions, garlic and tomatoes. Cover with more foil, then a lid. Heat until the smoke rises. Ram down the lid so no more smoke escapes. Smoke for 30–45 minutes, then remove from the heat and let cool, without lifting the lid.

Remove the tomatoes from the wok and press through a sieve. Stir in sea salt flakes to taste and keep hot.

Heat a grill pan over medium heat until hot, add the tuna and cook for 2 minutes until barred with brown and cooked 5 mm through. Turn the fish over and cook for another 2 minutes. It should be pink in the middle.

Lightly crush the beans with salt, pepper and reserved olive oil. Put piles of beans on 4 plates, add the tuna, onion wedges, garlic cloves and salad leaves. Drizzle with the smoked tomato sauce and serve.

Prawns always taste better if you cook them with their shells on, and it also improves their texture. When grilled, they are utterly sublime. I am a particular fan of Vietnamese flavours – their light, scented, salty, sweet, citrus notes are absolutely unbeatable.

char-grilled prawns
with vietnamese dipping sauce

4–6 large uncooked prawns per person

Chilli-lime marinade

4 tablespoons sunflower oil

2 tablespoons chilli oil

juice of 2 limes

1 tablespoon fish sauce

Nuóc cham

2 garlic cloves, sliced

1 red chilli, deseeded and sliced

1 tablespoon caster sugar

½ lime, deseeded and chopped (juice reserved)

1½ tablespoons fish sauce

Serves 4

To make the Nuóc Cham (Vietnamese dipping sauce), mash the garlic, chilli and sugar with a mortar and pestle, then mash in the lime flesh and juice. Transfer to a small bowl, stir in the fish sauce and 4 tablespoons water and set aside. Alternatively, mix the sugar, lime juice and fish sauce together, then stir in the sliced garlic, chilli and chopped lime.

If the prawns still have their heads, trim off all the whiskers and the ends of the legs. Rinse minimally (otherwise you'll rinse away all the flavour). Mix the marinade ingredients in a shallow dish, then add the prawns and turn to coat. Leave for 10–15 minutes, turning to coat. Heat a stove-top grill pan over medium heat to moderate.

Add the prawns to the pan and cook on both sides until the flesh is opaque and the shells scarlet and lightly charred, about 5 minutes. Do not overcook or the prawns will be tough.

Remove to a platter and serve with dipping bowls of Nuóc Cham.

thai aubergine salad
with prawns, oysters or mussels

6 Japanese or Chinese
   aubergines (the long thin
   ones) or 3 regular aubergines
1 large bunch of coriander
250 g peeled, cooked medium
   prawns, shucked oysters or
   shelled cooked mussels
peanut oil, for brushing

Thai dressing
60 g dried shrimps
grated zest and juice of 1 lime
   (2 tablespoons)
2 tablespoons fish sauce
1 stalk lemongrass, finely sliced
1 tablespoon brown sugar
3 red chillies, deseeded and
   chopped

Serves 4

This Thai way of cooking aubergines is delicious, and you can serve it with or without the seafood. It's much easier than the traditional way of cooking over an open flame (common in Thailand and the Middle East) – this way you avoid getting burnt bits of skin in the delicious smoky flesh. I use long thin aubergines for faster cooking (see the photograph on page 1).

Heat a stove-top grill pan over medium heat until hot. Put the aubergines in a plastic bag, add the oil, shake until well coated, then add to the pan and cook until charred on all sides. Remove from the pan, cut the aubergine in half and scrape the flesh into a serving bowl. Chop it into pieces. Add the prawns, oysters or mussels.

Put the dried shrimps in a food processor and blend until very fine. Mix the lime zest and juice, fish sauce, lemongrass, sugar, chillies and shrimp in a bowl, then pour over the aubergines and prawns. Top with the coriander and serve.

Microwave the green peas or broad beans on high for 2 minutes. Cool under running water, then transfer to a bowl of ice cubes and water. If using broad beans, pop them out of their grey skins, discard the skins and reserve the beans.

250 g shelled green peas or
  broad beans
about 20 scallops
green salad leaves
8 very finely cut slices smoked
  pancetta or streaky bacon
4 tablespoons extra virgin
  olive oil
4 teaspoons white rice vinegar
sea salt and freshly ground
  black pepper

Serves 4

Arrange the salad leaves on 4 plates.

Heat a stove-top grill pan or non-stick frying pan, add the pancetta and cook until crisp and brown on both sides. Drain on kitchen paper. Add the scallops to the pan and cook at a high heat for about 1 minute until browned on one side. Turn them over and brown the other side – about 1 minute. The scallops should be opaque all the way through. If not, continue cooking for about 1 minute more, or until opaque. Do not overcook or the scallops will shrink and be tough.

Meanwhile, divide the beans or peas and the bacon between each plate. As soon as the scallops are cooked, divide them between the plates, on top of the leaves. Pour the oil over the leaves, then sprinkle them with vinegar, salt and pepper. Serve with a dry white wine.

char-grilled scallop salad

A *salade tiède* (warm salad) of green leaves, crispy bacon and char-grilled scallops makes a delicious first course. It's important not to overcook scallops: cook them only until they become opaque (the time depends on their size). When you buy them, they should be creamy coloured. If they're white, they have been left to soak in water – they sponge up about 30 per cent of their own weight given half a chance – as soon as they hit the pan they drop it all and look limp and flaccid. You've paid good money for water!

paprika chicken wraps

Paprika chicken is one of my favourite ways with chicken. It adds extra pizzazz and deliciousness to any cut of chicken and suits this hybrid Mexican-cum-Middle Eastern serving method.

chicken and duck

4 chicken breasts
2 tablespoons olive oil
1 tablespoon paprika
1 teaspoon sea salt

To serve
lavash, pitta bread or village
    bread, warmed
cream cheese or hoummus
    (optional)
avocado (optional)
salad leaves
cherry tomatoes, halved
sea salt and freshly ground
    black pepper
juice of 1 lemon, plus 2 extra,
    halved, to serve (optional)

Serves 4

Split the chicken breasts through the thickness and open them out like a book. Put between 2 pieces of plastic and beat with the flat of a cleaver or tap all over with a rolling pin to thin out the breasts.

Put the breasts in a plastic bag and add the olive oil. Crush the paprika and salt with a small mortar and pestle, then add to the plastic bag. Shake and massage the chicken through the plastic bag, and leave for at least 30 minutes or overnight in the refrigerator.

When ready to cook, heat a stove-top grill pan over medium heat, then add the chicken and cook until nicely golden on one side, about 5 minutes. Turn them over and cook for about 5 minutes on the other side. Remove the chicken from the pan and slice into 1 cm wide strips.

To make the wraps, fold out the lavash or village bread, or open out the pitta. Add a dollop of cream cheese or hoummus and avocado, if using, then add the salad leaves, chicken strips and tomato halves. Add a squeeze of lemon juice, sprinkle with salt and pepper, roll up and serve. Serve extra lemon halves on the side.

tandoori chicken breasts

750 g boneless chicken breasts

First marinade

1 tablespoon salt
3 cm fresh ginger, grated
3 garlic cloves, crushed
2 tablespoons lemon juice

Second marinade

5 tablespoons grated
processed cheese
1 egg, beaten
2 red chillies, chopped
1 tablespoon Kashmiri chilli
powder or hot paprika
1 bunch of fresh coriander,
chopped
1 tablespoon wholemeal flour
½ cup single cream

To serve:

salad leaves
finely sliced red onion
lime wedges

Serves 4

Remove and discard the skin from the chicken breasts and cut the breasts in half through their thickness. Separate the 2 halves.

Put the ingredients for the first marinade in a shallow dish, and beat with a fork. Add the chicken breasts and turn to coat. Set aside for about 15–30 minutes.

Remove the chicken from the marinade and squeeze with your hands to remove excess moisture. Put all the ingredients for the second marinade in a blender and work to a purée. Transfer to a plastic bag, add the chicken and mix and knead the marinade into the chicken. Set aside for 30 minutes.

When ready to cook, heat a stove-top grill pan over medium heat. Remove the chicken from the bag. Put the chicken on the grill pan and cook for about 5 minutes on one side, without moving, then turn 45 degrees and cook for another 3 minutes. The breasts should be almost cooked through. Turn them over, turn the heat down and cook gently until the breasts are cooked through. Do not overcook or the chicken will be tough.

When the chicken is cooked, transfer to a serving plate and keep warm for about 5 minutes. Slice into wide strips.

Serve with salad leaves, sliced red onion and lime wedges.

The Indian tandoor is a clay oven that cooks at a hugely high temperature. Naan breads, slapped against its sides, cook in a matter of seconds. It is impossible to recreate the action of a tandoor in the domestic kitchen, but it is still possible to adapt the flavours and marinades to a more homely setting. This recipe is adapted from one given to me by the great chef Manjit Gill of the Bokhara Restaurant in the Maurya Sheraton Hotel in Delhi.

Pan-grilling is a good way to cook mild-tasting poussins – marinate them with your choice of Asian, Mexican, Italian or Middle Eastern flavours (this recipe is done with South African piri piri spices). Serve with your choice of vegetables, including any of the char-grilled ones in this book. This dish is perfect for two people: be ready with paper napkins or hot towels for cleaning up – this is definitely a hands-on dish.

piri piri spatchcocked poussins

2 poussins, spatchcocked*

Marinade
6 red chillies
3 garlic cloves
250 ml extra virgin olive oil
250 ml vodka

Piri piri sauce
6 red chillies
1 red onions, finely chopped
2 garlic cloves, crushed
1 bunch of fresh coriander, finely chopped
juice of 3 limes
sea salt

Serves 2

* To spatchcock (butterfly) the poussins, cut them down either side of the backbone with scissors or poultry shears. Discard the bone and press the bodies flat with the palm of your hand or a cleaver. You can also cut them in half completely – they will then fit more easily in your pan.

Mix the marinade ingredients together in a wide, flat bowl, add the poussins and turn to coat. Marinate for at least 30 minutes or overnight in the refrigerator. Turn the pieces at least once, and preferably more often, so the marinade can penetrate.

Put all the Piri Piri Sauce ingredients in a blender and blend. Transfer to a bowl and chill for at least 1 hour.

Heat a stove-top grill pan until hot. Remove the chicken from the marinade, then transfer to the pan. Put a plate on top and a heavy saucepan on top of that. Grill for 20 minutes, then turn over and baste with the marinade. Grill for another 10 minutes or until cooked through. Baste with the Piri Piri Sauce and serve with extra sauce.

Note: In South Africa, Piri Piri Chicken is one of the most popular takeaway dishes. Whole chickens are spatchcocked, then grilled on the barbecue. Piri Piri Sauce is splashed over them before they are chopped and bagged to take home. The sauce is Portuguese in ancestry, and found its way to South Africa via the former colonies of Angola and Mozambique.

Thai seven-spice is one of my favourite flavourings –
I use it as a dry rub for duck, chicken, meat and fish.
I buy it in the supermarket, but if you can't find it,
use Chinese five-spice powder instead.

Heat a stove-top grill pan over medium heat until hot. Make diagonal slices in the skin of the duck breasts, just through the skin and not cutting the meat. Add to the pan, skin side down, and cook at a medium heat until the fat runs and the skin is crispy, about 10 minutes. Pour off the fat as it accumulates in the pan (cool it and keep for another purpose such as frying potatoes).

4 duck breasts
4 teaspoons Thai 7-spice
2 teaspoons sea salt flakes

Char-grilled asparagus
250 g small asparagus spears
2 tablespoons peanut oil
sea salt and freshly ground
black pepper
Serves 4

Mix the 7-spice and salt together and brush over the flesh side of the duck breasts. Brush with some of the duck fat, then turn over the breasts and cook, flesh side down, for a further 5 minutes or until done (the time will depend on the thickness of the breasts). The breasts should be pink in the middle and crusty on the outside. Set aside in a warm place to set the juices while you prepare the rest of the dish.

Put the asparagus in a plastic bag, add the oil, salt and pepper and toss gently to coat with oil. Add to the pan and cook for about 5 minutes until lightly browned but still crisp.

To serve, cut the breasts crossways into slices about 1 cm thick. Divide the asparagus between 4 heated plates and add one sliced breast to each plate, keeping the slices together.

Thai seven-spice duck breasts

You can use any kind of meat for this dish – lamb or beef (chicken too). All over the Middle East and into Afghanistan and Pakistan, kebabs like these are cooked over long narrow open barbecues and served with the local flatbread – lavash, naan, village bread – whatever is the favourite in that area. The outdoor fire gives it a certain smokiness that's a little difficult to recreate in an ordinary kitchen, but a stove-top grill pan is a good start.

meat

persian meat kebabs

Trim the fat off the meat and cut the meat into small pieces, about 2–3 cm square. Put in a bowl, add the lemon juice, onions, garlic and a large pinch of salt. Mix well, cover and marinate in the refrigerator for at least 1 hour.

When ready to cook, mix in the egg, then thread the meat onto kebab skewers. Heat the grill pan over medium heat until hot. Add the kebabs and cook, without moving, for about 2 minutes or until crusty. Turn the kebabs over and cook the other side for another 2 minutes. Add the limes, cut side down, at the same time. Lamb and beef taste better a little rare – test one kebab to check it is done to your taste.

If you like, the marinated meat can be drained, minced in a food processor, then formed into balls which can be pressed onto the skewers. Serve with the grilled lime halves, minted yoghurt and flatbread.

1 kg lamb or beef
juice of 1 lemon
2 onions, grated
3 garlic cloves, crushed
1 egg, beaten
sea salt

To serve
4 limes, halved
250 ml plain yoghurt mixed with a
**   handful of chopped fresh mint**
flatbread such as lavash or pita bread

non-stick baking parchment
Serves 4

This alliance of Vietnamese marinated beef, crème fraîche, steamed sweet potatoes and a spicy Chilli Tomato Relish is a terrific combination and you can change the accent by choosing one of the marinades on pages 62–63.

4 slices fillet steak, each about 3 cm thick
4 small orange sweet potatoes, peeled and
    cut crossways into 2 cm thick slices

Marinade
2 tablespoons fish sauce
2 tablespoons mirin (Japanese rice wine)
1 tablespoon toasted sesame oil
grated zest and juice of 1 lime

Chilli tomato relish
250 g ripe tomatoes, skinned and chopped
250 g red peppers, peeled and chopped
6 red chillies, deseeded and chopped
7.5 cm fresh ginger, peeled and grated
2 tablespoons salt
200 g sugar
6 tablespoons sherry vinegar

To serve
a few handfuls of salad leaves
4 heaped tablespoons crème fraîche
Serves 4

To make the Chilli Tomato Relish, put all the ingredients in a food processor and pulse until coarsely chopped. Put in a saucepan, bring to the boil, skim off the foam, then reduce the heat and simmer for 30 minutes. Pour into hot sterilized jars, seal and let cool. Use immediately or store in the refrigerator: it will keep for 2 weeks.

Mix the marinade ingredients in a shallow dish. Add the beef, cover and set aside for at least 15 minutes. Turn over and marinate for at least another 15 minutes. Alternatively, chill overnight.

Heat a stove-top grill pan to medium-hot. Add the beef and cook for about 2 minutes on each side. The meat should be brown outside and rare in the middle. If you want it cooked further, cook for another 2 minutes for medium.

Meanwhile, steam the sweet potatoes until tender – or boil in salted water, then drain.

To serve, put a handful of leaves on each dinner plate, add a steak and a tumble of sweet potatoes, then a spoonful of crème fraîche and 1–2 tablespoons Chilli Tomato Relish.

pan-grilled vietnamese beef
with sweet potatoes, crème fraîche and chilli tomato relish

spicy lamburgers

Lamb makes marvellous, sweet burgers, but you may substitute the more traditional minced beef if you prefer. I first had these in India, where beef is forbidden, and have made them many times since. In any case, mince the meat yourself in a food processor, rather than buying it ready-minced. Since both lamb and beef are nicer a little rare, you can be sure that your own blades are perfectly clean and haven't been used to mince anything else.

1 kg boneless shoulder of lamb or beef, such
   as chuck, blade or flank
2 onions, finely chopped
2 garlic cloves, crushed
1 bunch of parsley, finely chopped

Spice mix
a pinch of ground allspice
a pinch of ground chillies
a pinch of nutmeg
a pinch of cinnamon
1/2 teaspoon salt
1 teaspoon freshly ground black pepper

To serve
fried onions
sliced tomato
sliced gherkins
Little Gem lettuce leaves
mustard or ketchup
toasted hamburger buns, buttered
Serves 4 or 6

Mince the lamb or beef in a food processor: there should be a good percentage of fat with the meat – at least 10 per cent – which will render out during cooking and keep the burger moist.

Mix the Spice Mix ingredients together in a small bowl. Put the lamb in a large bowl.

Put the onions in a bowl, cover with boiling water and set aside for 10 minutes. Drain and sprinkle the onion over the lamb. Sprinkle with the garlic, parsley and Spice Mix.

Knead the mixture with your hands, distributing the flavourings through the meat. Shape into 4–6 patties about 1.5 cm thick.

Heat a stove-top grill pan over medium heat until hot. Add the patties and cook, undisturbed, for 3–4 minutes – never press them down in the pan with a spatula. Turn them over and cook the other side for 3 minutes. Transfer to a plate and keep them warm.

Assemble the buns with lettuce, lamburgers, tomatoes, gherkins and fried onions, with mustard or ketchup to taste, then serve.

To make the Rosemary Oil, put the leaves from 2 of the rosemary sprigs and the garlic in a blender, add the olive oil and purée until chopped. Add the lemon zest and set aside for at least 1 hour, or overnight if possible, to infuse.

Cut the meat away from the end of the chop or cutlet bones, making clean bone 'handles'. Tuck small sprigs of rosemary and some lemon zest between meat and edge.

Heat a stove-top grill pan over medium heat until hot. Lightly brush the chops or cutlets with the Rosemary Oil, add to the pan and cook for 5 minutes without disturbing, then turn them over and cook for 3 minutes on the other side (or 5 minutes for medium). As the fat renders out of the meat, pour it off and discard – hold the chops in place with a spatula or a saucepan lid.

Meanwhile, par-boil the potatoes until almost tender, then drain, cut in half lengthways, brush with the Rosemary Oil and put, cut side down, on the grill pan. Cook for about 2 minutes until browned.

Transfer lamb and potatoes to heated dinner plates. Sprinkle with lemon juice, lemon zest, herb sprigs, salt and pepper, then serve.

12 lamb chops, with bones, or 16 lamb cutlets

zest and juice of 1 lemon

12 baby potatoes

sea salt and freshly ground black pepper

small sprigs of rosemary and thyme, to serve

Rosemary oil

6 sprigs of rosemary

3 garlic cloves, crushed

125 ml olive oil

zest of 1 lemon

Serves 4

Lamb is very well suited to the grill pan treatment. It is quite fatty meat, and as it cooks the fat renders out, leaving the meat tender and juicy. Pour off the fat from time to time (hold the lamb in place with a saucepan lid). Don't move the chops if you can help it – if you keep them still, they won't stick. Remember, don't oil the pan – if you're going to oil anything, oil the food.

rosemary lamb chops

char-grilled pork with aubergine

**4 large or 8 small pork chops,
    boneless, about 750 g
2 medium aubergines
peanut oil, for brushing**

Marinade
**125 ml fish sauce
2 tablespoons kecap manis
    (Indonesian sweetened soy
    sauce) or soy sauce
4 tablespoons sake or vodka
1 tablespoon chilli oil**

To serve
**garlic mashed potatoes
mustard and cress
oven-roasted tomato halves**
Serves 4

Put all the marinade ingredients in a wide, shallow dish, add the pork chops and turn to coat. Cover and chill for 1 hour or overnight, turning from time to time in the marinade.

When ready to cook, heat a large stove-top grill pan over medium heat until hot. If your pan is small, cook the aubergines first, keep them warm in the oven, then cook the pork chops.

Cut the aubergines lengthways into slices about 1 cm thick. Add the pork chops to the grill pan. Dip each slice of aubergine in the marinade and add to the grill pan in a single layer. Brush the chops and aubergine with marinade and leave, without disturbing, for about 5 minutes.

Brush the chops and aubergines with marinade again and turn them over to cook the other side. Brush the cooked side of the aubergines with peanut oil. Leave for another 5 minutes, or until the chops are cooked through.

Meanwhile, cook the potatoes and garlic in boiling salted water until tender. Drain, let steam dry for 2 minutes, then mash and beat in the butter and milk.

To serve, put a dollop of mashed potatoes on each plate and put a pork chop on top. Arrange a share of the char-grilled aubergine on top, arranging each slice at 90 degrees to the previous one. Add 2–3 oven-roasted tomato halves, sprinkle with mustard and cress and serve.

If you have much marinade left over, bring it to the boil, simmer for 3 minutes, then drizzle over the dish.

Based on the Vietnamese and other South-east Asian flavours that I love, this marinade began as a flavour-enhancer for pork, but I discovered how good it is with aubergine more or less by mistake. Its great advantage is that it flavours and tenderizes without the usual blotting paper absorption that you get when you put oil anywhere near an aubergine.

jerk pork

Jerk seasoning can be applied to pork, chicken or seafood to make what are probably the most famous Caribbean dishes – serve it with roti, hardoe or bulla, the delicious Jamaican breads. A crisp and creamy salsa goes well with the spicy jerk flavours.

4 tablespoons allspice berries

6 spring onions, chopped

2 hot red chillies, deseeded

3 garlic cloves, crushed

leaves from 4 sprigs of thyme

2 dried bay leaves, crumbled

**sea salt and freshly ground
  black pepper**

4–8 pork chops

**4 buns such as hardoe, bulla or
  bun or roti, or crusty bread,
  to serve**

Avocado salsa

**1 ripe Hass avocado, scooped
  out with a teaspoon**

5 cm cucumber, diced

4 small plum tomatoes, diced

1 red chilli, diced

4 limes, halved

**sea salt and freshly ground
  black pepper**

Serves 4

To make the Jerk Seasoning, put the allspice in a dry frying pan and heat for about 5 minutes. Transfer to a clean coffee grinder. Grind to a powder, then add the thyme and bay leaves and grind again. Add the spring onions, chillies, garlic, salt and pepper and grind to a paste. You can also use a blender, but the dry spices should be pounded in a mortar and pestle first.

Press the spice paste into the pork and set aside for about 2 hours or overnight in the refrigerator. When ready to cook, heat a stove-top grill pan over medium heat, add the pork and cook at a medium heat for about 15 minutes. Do not overheat or the spices will burn. Turn the meat over and cook for another 15 minutes or until cooked through.

Grill the buns or bread on the grill pan until toasty.

To make the salsa, put the avocado, cucumber, tomatoes, chilli, salt and pepper in a bowl. Stir in the juice of 2 limes. Serve the salsa with the chops, grilled buns or bread and remaining limes, cut in half.

marinades and rubs

Marinades and rubs appear throughout this book, but here are some more. What's the difference? A marinade is liquid and a rub is dry. Add oils, rubs and marinades to the food – not the pan. Be careful adding salty ingredients, such as soy and fish sauce, too early in preparation: salt draws out moisture and can make the food dry, though it also intensifies flavours. Acid ingredients, such as citrus juice or vinegar also have a rather energetic effect: they can cook seafood on their own, and start to break down the flesh of poultry and meats.

Italian Marinade
4 tablespoons olive oil
4 tablespoons red or white wine
4 tablespoons orange juice
a handful of fresh herbs, chopped

Chinese Marinade
3 cm fresh ginger, grated
4 spring onions, finely chopped
4 tablespoons soy sauce
2 tablespoons honey
2 whole star anise, crushed

South-east Asian Marinade
125 ml fish sauce
4 tablespoons sake or vodka
1 tablespoon chilli oil

Vietnamese Marinade
4 tablespoons fish sauce
4 tablespoons mirin
1 tablespoon sesame oil
5 cm fresh ginger, grated

Ginger Marinade
2 tablespoons peanut oil
2 cm fresh ginger, grated
1 tablespoon vodka
2 teaspoons 5-spice powder
1 teaspoon sea salt flakes
1 tablespoon chilli oil

Moroccan Yellow Marinade
½ teaspoon ground ginger
2 teaspoons saffron powder
a pinch of cumin (optional)
2 tablespoons olive oil

For all the above marinades, put the ingredients in a shallow dish, stir with a fork, then add the main ingredient and infuse for at least 30 minutes, or overnight, covered, in the refrigerator.

A rub is a dry seasoning, often no more than salt and pepper, though it usually contains spices of some kind. This can be a trap, because spices burn easily.

My solution is to apply the rub on one side only – the meaty side, as in the duck breasts on page 42. Leave to penetrate for as long as possible, then cook the other side. When the food is almost cooked through, turn it over and cook the rubbed side, reducing the heat a little to prevent the spices burning.

This is particularly important for rubs containing salt: salt draws moisture out of the salted object, so it can become less juicy, not more so. The exception is the Japanese method of salting fish (page 23), which draws the juices through and towards the skin, making the flesh firm and delicious.

Paprika Butter
1 tablespoon sweet paprika
½ teaspoon cumin
4 tablespoons butter

Saffron Pepper
2 sachets saffron powder or
   2 large pinches of saffron
   threads, toasted in a dry pan,
   then crushed
3 cm grated ginger or
   1 teaspoon ground ginger
1 tablespoon cracked black pepper

Moroccan Garlic Rub

3 garlic cloves, crushed
5 cm fresh ginger, grated
½ teaspoon cumin seeds
   (optional)
2 tablespoons sweet paprika
1 teaspoon ground cinnamon
1 teaspoon cracked black pepper
2 teaspoons ground coriander
1 teaspoon salt
2 tablespoons brown sugar

Paprika Salt

1 tablespoon sweet or hot paprika
1 teaspoon sea salt

For all the above rubs, mix all the ingredients together and rub all over or on one side only of the meat, fish or poultry.

Chilli Rub

1 teaspoon ground cumin
1 tablespoon ground coriander
2 teaspoons mustard seeds
4 tablespoons sweet paprika
4 tablespoons Kashmiri or ancho
   chilli powder
1 tablespoon sea salt
1 tablespoon freshly ground
   black pepper

Put the cumin, coriander and mustard seeds in a dry frying pan and heat until aromatic and the seeds begin to pop. Remove from the heat and crush with a mortar and pestle. Mix with the remaining ingredients and use as a rub. Store any leftovers in a screwtop jar in the refrigerator.

fruits

Many fruits are suited to grilling – the heat brings out their sweetness and flavour. I like to brush the cut surface with honey so it becomes even more caramelized. The Passionfruit Galliano is optional, but it is delicious and the only known use for Galliano other than in a Harvey Wallbanger!

4 ripe purple figs, halved lengthways
4 nectarines, peaches or apricots, halved and pitted
honey, for brushing

Passionfruit galliano
4 ripe passionfruit
2 tablespoons Galliano or Grand Marnier

Vanilla mascarpone
3 cardamom pods
¼ teaspoon vanilla extract
250 ml mascarpone
1 tablespoon icing sugar
Serves 4

Scrape the passionfruit flesh into a cup or bowl, stir in the Galliano and set aside.

To make the Vanilla Mascarpone, put the cardamom pods in a mortar and crush with a pestle. Discard the green pods and crush the black seeds more. Add the vanilla and crush again. Let steep while you whip the mascarpone and icing sugar together. Stir in the cardamom-vanilla mixture and set aside.

Brush the cut sides of the figs and nectarines with honey and put, cut side down, on a preheated grill pan. Cook for about 3 minutes until barred golden-brown and heated through, but not mushy. Transfer to 4 small heated plates. Add spoonfuls of the mascarpone mixture, then drizzle with spoonfuls of Passionfruit Galliano.

grilled figs and nectarines
with vanilla mascarpone and cardamom seeds

grilled sugar bananas
with cinnamon, rum and lime ice cream

Street hawkers in Thailand sell grilled bananas in a dozen different guises. I love the tiny sugar bananas, also known as ladies' fingers, shown here – I bought them in an Indian market, but where I grew up, they were the preferred variety. The ice cream is based on the delicious Spanish drink, *leche merengada* – made with lime and rum, rather than lemon.

6 small bananas, such as sugar bananas, ladies' fingers or apple bananas, or 4 regular bananas, unpeeled, halved lengthways
honey, for brushing

Rum and lime ice cream
1 litre full-cream milk
335 g sugar
peeled or grated zest of 2 limes
1 cinnamon stick, broken into pieces
4 tablespoons dark rum
2 egg whites (optional)

To serve
finely grated zest of 2 limes
4 pinches ground cinnamon
Serves 4

To make the Rum and Lime Ice Cream, put the milk, sugar, lime zest and broken cinnamon stick in a saucepan and bring to the boil, stirring. Boil for 2 minutes, then remove from the heat and let cool. Strain and discard the solids. Stir in the rum. Churn in an ice cream maker or freeze in a plastic container. If the latter, when frozen, beat with a hand-held stick blender until thick and creamy. If using egg whites, beat them to a froth, then blend into the mixture.

Freeze the ice cream – it can be kept frozen for some time, but has better texture if eaten within a week.

To grill the bananas, brush the cut sides with honey and put, cut side down, on a pre-heated stove-top grill pan. Cook for about 5 minutes, then turn them over and cook the other side – the time will depend on the thickness of the bananas. To test, prick with a fork: the flesh should be hot and creamy.

To serve, arrange 2–3 banana halves on each plate, cut side up and ends overlapping. Add 2 large scoops of ice cream, sprinkle with grated lime zest and a little cinnamon, then serve.

Pavlova
4 egg whites
a pinch of salt
250 g caster sugar
1 tablespoon cornflour
2 teaspoons white wine vinegar
1 teaspoon vanilla extract

Grilled fruit
2 tablespoons rum
4 tablespoons honey
4 large, ripe mangoes
8 pineapple rings

Fruit salad
1 pink papaya, peeled, halved, deseeded and cubed
6 large strawberries, quartered
juice of ½ orange
1 tablespoon icing sugar

To serve
250 ml double cream
1 tablespoon icing sugar
a few drops of vanilla extract
flesh of 2–6 passionfruit

a large baking sheet
baking parchment, buttered and dusted with cornflour
Serves 6–8

Pavlova is a pudding made in heaven. It is the national dish of both Australia and New Zealand and the two countries are locked in battle to claim credit for its invention. In fact it's not unlike several classic French confections, but it is the tropical fruits that make it special.

To make the pavlova, put the egg whites in a dry, warm bowl and add a pinch of salt. Beat until soft peaks form. Add half the sugar, 1 tablespoon at a time. Fold in the remaining sugar and sprinkle in the cornflour. Stir in the vinegar and vanilla.

Put the prepared baking parchment on a baking sheet, add the mixture and spread to a circle about 20 cm across. Cook in a preheated oven at 150°C (300°F) Gas 2 for 1 hour and 15 minutes.*

Put the fruit salad ingredients in a bowl, stir and leave to infuse for 30 minutes. Put the cream, icing sugar and vanilla in a medium bowl and whip softly.

Mix the rum and honey together. Peel the mangoes and cut off the cheeks. Brush the pineapple rings and mango cheeks with rum and honey. Preheat a stove-top grill pan to medium, add the mango and pineapple and cook until lightly barred with brown on both sides – the heat brings out the flavour. Remove from the heat and cut into 1–2 cm pieces.

Put the pineapple and mango in the pavlova, spoon over the fruit salad and top with whipped cream, passionfruit and any fruit salad juice. Serve in wedges.

*Note: If pavlovas and meringues are cooked in an electric or fan-assisted oven, they will be white. If cooked in a gas oven, they will be a pale, pinkish-fawn.

papaya and passionfruit pavlova
with pan-grilled pineapple and mango

index